CW01676612

Contents

Scope and sequence

	Vocabulary	Grammar	Global Citizenship	Project	My sounds
Welcome to the Rise and Shine Explorers Club	**Numbers 11-20; days of the week:** Monday, Tuesday, Wednesday, Thursday, Friday, Saturday, Sunday **School items:** pen, rubber, ruler, notebook	It's (Monday). It's (rainy). What's this / that? This is my (pen). That's your (ruler). How many (pencils)? (Twelve).	**Let's be explorers!**	**My Explorers Club passport**	**th (voiced), th (voiceless)**
1 Let's explore together	**My things:** backpack, belt, cap, coat, glasses, scarf, trainers, watch **Adjectives:** dark, fair, long, short	Have you got (a watch)? Yes, I have. / No, I haven't. He/she's got (glasses).	**Our local heroes:** builder, chef, explorer, teacher	**A club book**	**w, y**
2 Let's be happy at home **Review 1** Important to me	**House:** bathroom, bedroom, garage, garden, hall, kitchen, living room, stairs **Furniture:** bed, lamp, sofa, table	Where's (Peanut)? He's in (the garden). Where's (the lamp)? It's (next to/on) (the table).	**Unusual homes:** cave, igloo, tent, treehouse	**A perfect house**	**r, l**
3 Let's explore nature	**Farm animals:** chicken, cow, donkey, goat, goose, horse, sheep, turkey **Outdoors:** bush, fence, rock, wall	There's (a horse). There isn't (a cow). Where's (the cow)? It's (behind) (the wall).	**The five senses:** hear, see, smell, taste, touch	**A five senses park map**	**oo, ee**
4 Let's try new activities **Review 2** All about me	**Actions:** catch, climb, kick, ride, skate, skip, swim, swing **Activities with *play*:** a board game, football, the guitar, tennis	Can you (skip)? Yes, I can. / No, I can't. But I can (swim). Can (he) play (tennis)? Yes, (he) can. / No, (he) can't.	**Musical instruments:** drums, piano, recorder, violin	**A club**	**a, i**
5 Let's share our food	**Food:** biscuit, burger, carrot, cereal, egg, fish, juice, orange **Verbs:** cook, grow, make, wash	What are you doing? I'm (eating). Are you (cooking)? Yes, I am. / No, I'm not.	**Food and ingredients:** butter, flour, fruit, vegetables	**A food truck bar**	**i, o**
6 Let's have holiday fun **Review 3** Around me	**Holiday activities:** build a sandcastle, collect shells, go on holiday, play on the beach, read comics, sleep **Time of day:** morning, afternoon, evening, night	I want to (build a sandcastle). Do you want to (play the guitar) (in the morning)? Yes, I do. / No, I don't.	**Water safety:** safe, sea, dangerous, flag	**A holiday trip**	**u, e**
Goodbye	**Happy holidays!**				
Celebrations	**Let them shine:** balloon, barbecue, cake, candle, present, sparkler **Beautiful world!:** desert, hill, jungle, mountain, ocean, sky **Amazing oceans:** dolphin, octopus, seahorse, seal, shark, whale **Let them fly!:** cloud, day, moon, night, star, sun				

My Progress Chart

	Welcome	Unit 1	Unit 2	Unit 3	Unit 4	Unit 5	Unit 6
Listening	I can recognise my words.	I can hear my words in dialogues.		I can listen to descriptions and information.		I can understand my phrases and sentences in dialogues.	
Reading	I can recognise my words.	I can recognise my phrases and sentences in short stories.		I can read short stories and descriptions.		I can read short stories and notice detailed information.	
Speaking	I can say my words and phrases.	I can describe people and things.		I can ask and answer questions about the world around me.		I can talk about myself and my world.	
Writing	I can make marks and write numbers.	I can trace and copy my words.		I can write my words and phrases.		I can write my sentences.	

Welcome to the Rise and Shine Explorers Club

Lesson 1

Who do you know?

1 Listen and explore. 0.04

Rise and shine,
It's a beautiful day.
Open your eyes,
Let's learn and play!

Tell me!
What's your friend's name?

2 Point, trace and say.

3 Write your name.

Lesson 2

1 0.05 Sing and act. **Song**

1, 2, 3, 4, 5, 6, 7, 8, 9, 10,
11, 12, 13, 14, 15, 16, 17, 18, 19, 20!
Hooray! Hooray! Let's explore today!
Monday, Tuesday, Wednesday, Thursday
Friday, Saturday, Sunday!
Hooray! Hooray! Let's explore today!

2 0.07 Listen again and read. Tick (✓) and say.

MONDAY	WEDNESDAY	FRIDAY	SATURDAY
13	15	17	18
☐	☐	☐	☐

I can shine!

3 Choose and say.

Thirteen!

It's Monday!

I can recognise days of the week and numbers up to 20.

Lesson 3

1 0.08 Listen, point and say.

windy

rainy

sunny

cloudy

2 0.09 Listen or watch.

Let's imagine!

Draw your favourite weather.

I can shine!

One. It's cloudy.

3 Look at the story. Number and say.

 ☐

 ☐

 ☐

 ☐

I can read a story about the weather.

Lesson 4 and 5

1 0.10 Listen and find.

2 0.11 Listen, read and say.

Chant

What's this?
This is my pen.
What's that?
That's my ruler.

This is my pen.
That's your ruler.

3 0.12 Listen and say.
Then write.

My sounds

This and that!
Thank you! Thank you!

I can shine!

4 Play!

I can ask and answer about objects.

Lesson 6 and 7

1 0.14 Listen, write and say.

11 eleven | 12 twelve | 13 thirteen | 14 fourteen | 15 fifteen

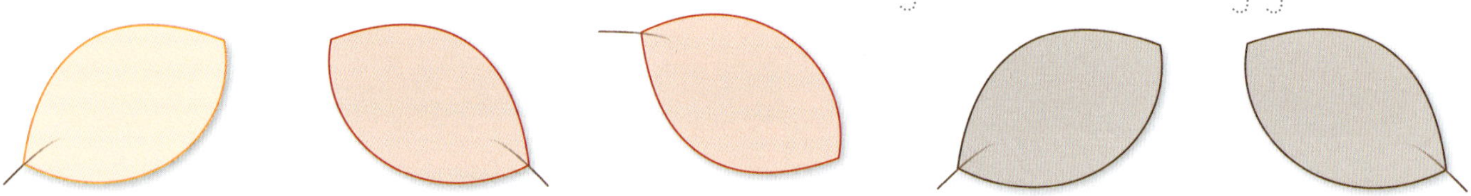

16 sixteen | 17 seventeen | 18 eighteen | 19 nineteen | 20 twenty

2 Count and write.

1  ______

2  ______

3 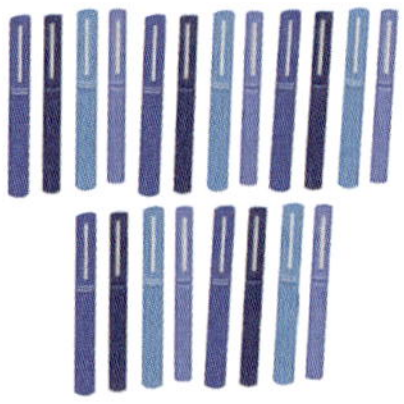 ______

4 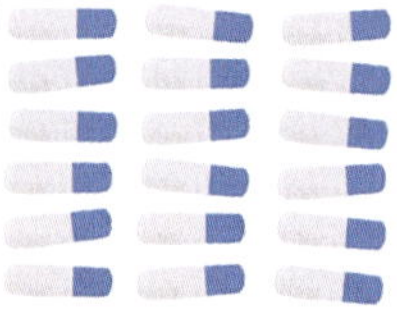 ______

Think and share!

Can you count in twos?
10 … 12 … 14 …

I can shine!

3 Play!

How many pencils?

Twelve!

I can ask and answer about how many.

My Explorers Club passport

Review

1 Complete.

Favourite day	I like	I've got	Favourite number
Monday			
Tuesday			
Wednesday			
Thursday			
Friday			
Saturday			
Sunday			

My name is ______________________

I'm ______________________.

The Rise and Shine Explorers Club

Time to shine!

2 Show and say.

My name is Sam. I'm 8. My favourite day is Saturday. I like tomatoes. I've got a brother. My favourite number is twenty!

Welcome

Let's explore together!

1 Let's explore together

Lesson 1

Where are the children?

1 1.01 Listen and explore.

Tell me!
What have you got in your classroom?

2 1.02 Listen, stick and say.

3 Trace and read.

4 Watch and listen.

I've got a cap.

Lesson 2

1 1.03 Sing and act. Song

Have you got a backpack and a watch?
Yes, I have. Yes, I have.
Have you got trainers and a coat?
Yes, I have. Yes, I have.
Have you got glasses and a scarf?
Yes, I have. Yes, I have.
Have you got a belt and a cap?
No, I haven't. No, I haven't.

2 1.05 Listen and tick (✓) or cross (✗). Say.

Have you got a scarf?
Yes, I have. / No, I haven't.

I can shine!

3 Ask and answer.

Have you got a watch?

Yes, I have!

I can name my things.

Lesson 3

1 How many? Look at the story. Count and write the number.

belts ☐

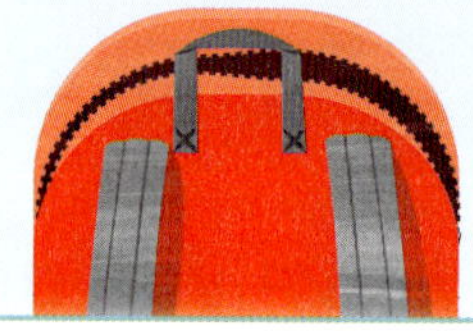
backpacks ☐

caps ☐

2 1.07 Listen or watch.

I can shine!

3 Circle the club mascot.

a frog

a cat

a butterfly

a rabbit

4 Act out.

I can understand a story about choosing a club mascot.

Let's imagine!

What has the club got?
Is Peanut happy?

Lesson 4

1 1.08 Listen and find.

2 1.09 Listen and number. Say.

3 1.10 Listen, read and say.

She's got long hair.

Chant

She's got long hair.
He's got short hair.
She's got dark hair.
He's got fair hair.

4 Read and match. Then say.

1

David

2

Sonia

3

Veronica

4

Teo

a She's got long, fair hair.

b He's got short, fair hair.

c He's got short, dark hair.

d She's got long, dark hair.

Lesson 5

1 1.11 Listen and match.

2 Look and play. Add one more.

She's got a short coat and new glasses.

She's got a long belt, too. Blue backpack!

3 1.12 Listen, write and say.

My sounds

It's windy! Look at your yellow watch!

I can shine!

4 Cut out, choose and play.

Have you got glasses?

She's got glasses.

Yes, I have.

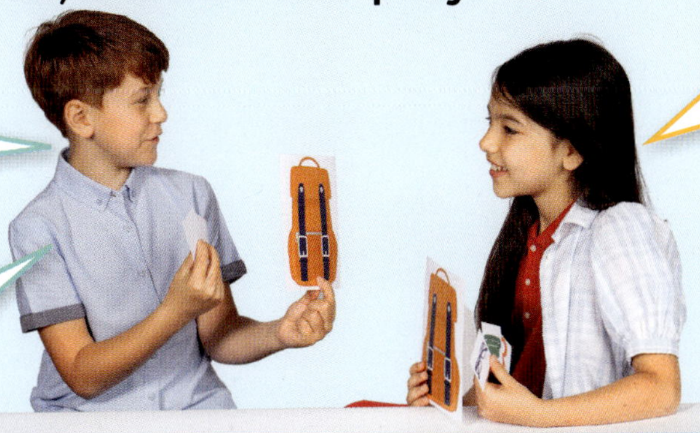

I can describe my friends and talk about what they've got.

Lesson 6

1 1.15 Listen, look and find.

2 1.16 Listen, point and say.

3 Circle the odd one out.

1 a  b  c 

2 a  b  c 

3 a  b  c 

Think and share!
Who's a hero in your community?

4 Watch and listen.

Lesson 7

Commenting on a photo

1 1.17 Listen and write. Then read and number.

1. He's a ______________.
2. She's a ______________.
3. He's an ______________.
4. She's a ______________.

What a great photo!

2 Read. Then write.

Back Likes 21 Comments 1

posted by Oscar123

This is me and my neighbours.
It's our street party.

Comments

posted by ClaraT

What a ______________

______________!

I can shine!

3 Take a photo and say.

Look at this!

Oh, what a great photo!

I can comment on a photo.

Let's make a club book!

Step 1 Review

1 Find and write.

2 Look, think and tick (✓) for you. Ask and answer.

coat scarf glasses belt watch backpack cap trainers

1 ______________ ☐
2 ______________ ☐
3 ______________ ☐
4 ______________ ☐
5 ______________ ☐
6 ______________ ☐
7 ______________ ☐
8 ______________ ☐

Have you got glasses?

Yes, I have.

3 Play!

She's got long, fair hair. She's got a big, yellow watch. Who is it?

It's Anna!

4 Think! Who's in your club? Write and say.

__________ is in my club.

Step 2 Create

5 Think about your friends. What have they got? Tick (✓).

☐

☐

☐

☐

6 Make a club book. Draw or take photos. Write.

7 Describe your friend.

Look! This is Zana.

Time to shine!

8 Share your club book with the class.

I appreciate my friends and community.

2 Let's be happy at home

Lesson 1

Where are the children?

1 2.01 Listen and explore.

Tell me!
Where do you live?

2 2.02 Listen, stick and say.

3 Trace and read.

4 Watch and listen.

Lesson 2

1 2.03 **Sing and act.** Song

Where's Peanut?
In the kitchen or the living room?
In the bathroom or the bedroom?
In the garage or on the stairs?
Where's Peanut?
He's in the garden!
Yes! Yes! Yes!

2 2.05 **Listen and match. Say.**

1 Mum 2 Dad 3 Granny

Where's Mum?
She's in the living room.

I can shine!

3 **Ask and answer.**

Where's Clara?

She's in the garden.

I can name places in a house.

Lesson 3

1 Look at the story. Where is Clara? Tick (✓).

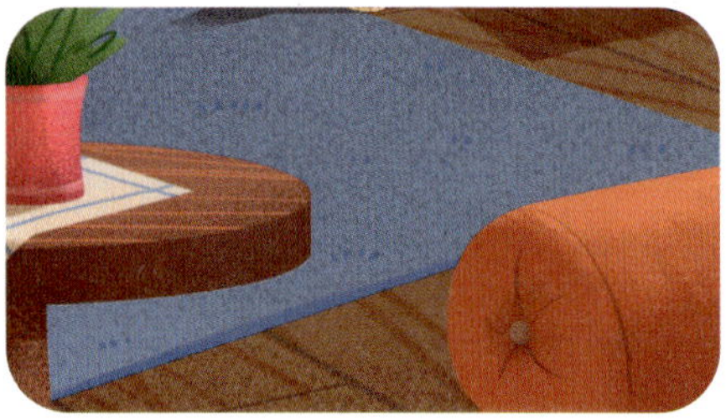

living room ☐

kitchen ☐

garden ☐

2 2.07 Listen or watch.

Let's imagine!

What can you do to feel happy at home?

I can shine!

3 Who has a bedroom in the garden? Read and circle.

Basil Peanut Clara

4 Act out.

I can understand a story about places in a house.

Lesson 4

1 2.08 Listen and find. **2** 2.09 Listen and number. Say.

3 2.10 Listen, read and say.

Where's the table?
It's next to the bed.

Chant

Where's the lamp? It's on the table.
Where's the table? It's next to the bed.

4 Circle four differences. Choose, write and say.

Where's ________________?

It's ________________.

Where's ________________?

It's ________________.

Lesson 5

1 2.11 Listen and match.

1 
2 
3 

a 
b 
c 

2 Look and play. Add one more.

Where's the lamp?

It's in the bedroom. It's on the table.

3 2.12 Listen, write and say.

My sounds

A red lamp in the living room.

I can shine!

4 Cut out, fold and play.

Where's the cat?

It's in the bedroom. It's on the bed!

I can say where things are in my house.

Lesson 6

1 2.15 Listen, look and find.

2 2.16 Listen, point and say.

3 Which home? Look and write. Say.

1 ______________________

2 ______________________

3 ______________________

4 ______________________

1 

2 

3 

4 

4 Watch and listen.

Think and share!

What makes a home?

Lesson 7

Making suggestions

1 Read. Then listen and write. 2.17

To do list

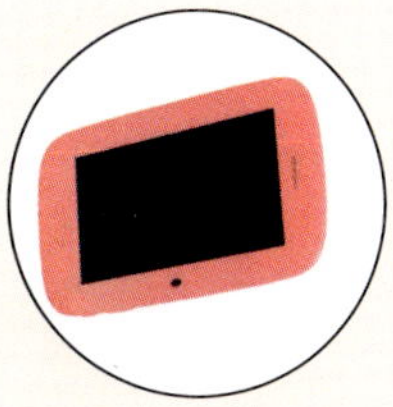

1. tablet on the ______________________
2. backpack on the ____________________
3. pyjamas on the _____________________

2 Choose and write.

pencils books rulers
rubbers notebooks

To do list

____

____

____

I can shine!

3 Tidy your desk. Say.

I can make a suggestion.

Let's design a perfect house

Step 1 Review

bathroom bedroom living room
kitchen stairs hall garden garage

1 Look and write.

1

____

2

____

3

____

4

____

5

____

6

____

7

____

8

____

2 Look and circle. Ask and answer.

Where's the cat? It's in the garden / living room.

Where's the fish? It's in the kitchen / bedroom.

3 Play!

Where's the lamp?

It's on the table.

4 What's your favourite room? Write.

I like my ____________________.

Step 2 Create

5 Which homes do you like? Tick (✓) or cross (✗).

6 Make a plan of your perfect house.

7 Decide where to put things in your house.

Let's put the lamp on the table.

Good idea!

Time to shine!

8 Share your house design with the class.

It's a tent house. This is the living room. The sofa is next to the table.

What a great house!

I care about my home.

Review 1 Important to me

1 Listen and number. 2.18

2 Look and point. Then ask and answer.

3 Read and write.

living room bedroom garden

1 Where's the  ? It's in the ____________________.

2 Where's the  ? It's in the ____________________.

3 Where's the  ? It's in the ____________________.

Mini-project

4 Complete the checklist for you.

Have you got a backpack?

He's got a watch.

Where's the coat?

Time to shine!

5 Read and tick (✓).

1 I can read and write words about homes and things.

2 I can talk about my home and my things.

3 I can comment on a photo.

4 I can say where things are.

6 Vote. Say and sing.

My favourite song is	____________ ____________
My favourite new word is	____________ ____________

3 Let's explore nature

Lesson 1

Where are the children?

1 3.01 Listen and explore.

Tell me!
What animals are there where you live?

2 3.02 Listen, stick and say.

3 Trace and read.

4 Watch and listen.

Lesson 2

1 3.03 **Sing and act.** Song

There isn't a fox or a duck or a turtle
On the farm, on the farm, on the city farm!
There's a cow and a donkey and a horse, too
On the farm, on the farm, on the city farm!
There's a chicken and a goose and a turkey, too.
On the farm, on the farm! (x2)
On the city farm!
There's a sheep and a goat, all for you!
On the farm, on the farm, on the city farm!
On the city farm!

2 3.05 **Listen and tick (✓).**

a

b

There's a goose and a turkey.
There isn't a frog.

I can shine!

3 **Choose, think and say.**

It's got four legs. It's white.

A sheep! There's a sheep on the farm!

I can name farm animals.

Lesson 3

1 How many animals? Look at the story. Count and write the number.

four legs ☐ two legs ☐

2 3.07 Listen or watch.

 Story value A story about making animals happy

Let's imagine!

Where's Peanut? How do you think he feels?

I can shine!

3 Read and match.

1  2  3 

horses chickens goats

4 Act out.

I can understand a story about farm animals.

Lesson 4

1 3.08 Listen and find. **2** 3.09 Listen and number. Say.

3 3.10 Listen, read and say.

Where's the cow?
It's behind the wall.

Chant

Where's the cow? It's behind the wall.
Is there a horse behind the wall?
No, there isn't! There's a cow behind the wall!

4 Follow and find. Write and say.

Where's the goat?

It's behind the wall.

1 There's a ______________ behind the ______________.

2 There's a ______________ behind the ______________.

3 There's a ______________ behind the ______________.

Lesson 5

1 3.11 Listen and number. Say.

2 Look and play. Add one more.

There's a fox on the farm.

Where's the chicken?

It's behind the rock.

Picture c!

3 3.12 Listen, write and say.

My sounds

A goose with boots.
A sheep with teeth!

I can shine!

4 Cut out, play and say.

I can ask and answer about what there is on a farm.

Lesson 6

1 (3.15) Listen, look and find. **2** (3.16) Listen, point and say.

3 Look and read. Tick (✓) or cross (✗). Then say.

see				
touch				
hear				
taste				
smell				

I can taste an apple!

Think and share!
What's your favourite smell?

4 Watch and listen.

Lesson 7

Asking for and giving information

1 3.17 Read and number. Listen and check.

a There's a café next to the garden. ☐

b There's a pond behind the trees. ☐

c There's a playground behind the café. ☐

d There's a city farm next to the playground. ☐

2 Read and complete.

1  The ______ is next to the garden.

2  The ______ is next to the playground.

3  The ______ is behind the café.

I can shine!

3 Ask and answer.

I can give information.

Let's make a five senses park map!

Step 1 Review

1 Look and write.

goat cow horse chicken goose donkey turkey sheep

1 ______________
2 ______________
3 ______________
4 ______________
5 ______________
6 ______________
7 ______________
8 ______________

2 Look, choose and complete. Then say.

There's a ______________ behind the ______________.

3 Ask and answer.

Where's the goat?

It's behind the rock.

4 Think! What's your favourite outdoor space near your house?

I like ____.

Step 2 Create

5 What can you do in your park? Tick (✓) or cross (✗).

6 Make a map of your park. Draw and write.

7 Describe your park.

Look! There's a turkey. It's behind the flowers.

Time to shine!

8 Share your map with the class.

I explore nature.

4 Let's try new activities

Lesson 1

Where are the children?

1 4.01 Listen and explore.

Tell me!

What's your favourite thing to do?

2 4.02 Listen, stick and say.

3 Trace and read.

4 Watch and listen.

Lesson 2

1 4.03 **Sing and act.** Song

Can you ride a bike, can you catch a ball?
Can you skate, can you climb a wall?
Can you swing and swim, can you kick a ball?
No, I can't! No, I can't. (x2)
Try! Try! Try! (x2)

Can you ride a bike? No, I can't.
Can you catch a ball? No, I can't.
Can you skate? No, I can't.
Can you climb a wall? No, I can't.
Can you swing and swim? No, I can't.
Can you kick a ball? No, I can't.
Try! Try! Try! (x2)
Yes, I can!

2 4.05 **Listen and tick (✓) or cross (✗). Say.**

Can you swim?
Yes, I can. / No, I can't.

I can shine!

3 **Ask and answer.**

Can you skip?

No, I can't.
But I can swim!

I can name physical activities.

Lesson 3

1 Look at the story. Who can swim? Tick (✓).

Tess ☐ Oscar ☐ Clara ☐ Basil ☐

2 4.07 Listen or watch.

Rise and Shine Explorers Club

Let's imagine!

What does Oscar want to do?

I can shine!

3 Read. Then write T (True) or F (False).

1 Oscar can swing. He helps Peanut. ☐

2 Tess can climb. She helps Peanut. ☐

3 Clara can swim. She helps Peanut. ☐

4 Act out.

I can understand a story about different activities.

Lesson 4

1 4.08 Listen and find. **2** 4.09 Listen and number. Say.

3 4.10 Listen, read and say.

Can he play tennis?
Yes, he can. / No, he can't.

Chant

Can she play tennis? Yes, she can!
Can he play football? No, he can't!
But he can play the guitar. Yes, he can!

4 Ask and answer. Complete. Then say.

My friend				
______	 ☐	 ☐	 ☐	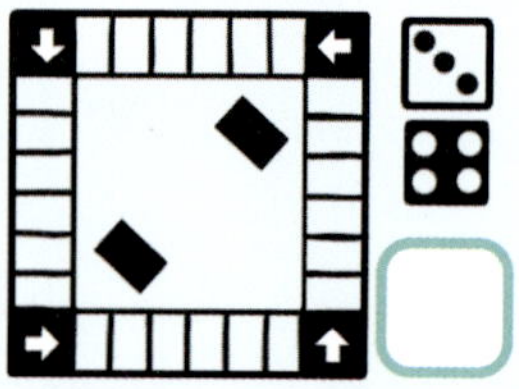 ☐

Can he / she play football? ______, ______ ______.

Can he / she play a board game? ______, ______ ______.

Lesson 5

1 4.11 Listen and tick (✓) or cross (✗). Say.

2 Look and play. Add one more.

Can he play tennis?

No, he can't but he can skate!

3 4.12 Listen, write and say.

My sounds

She can't ride a bike but she can play a game!

I can shine!

4 Cut out, write and play.

I can ask and answer about what others can do.

Lesson 6

1 Listen, look and find. (4.15)

2 Listen and number. (4.16)

violin ☐

drums ☐

piano ☐

recorder ☐

3 Read and tick (✓).

How do we play?

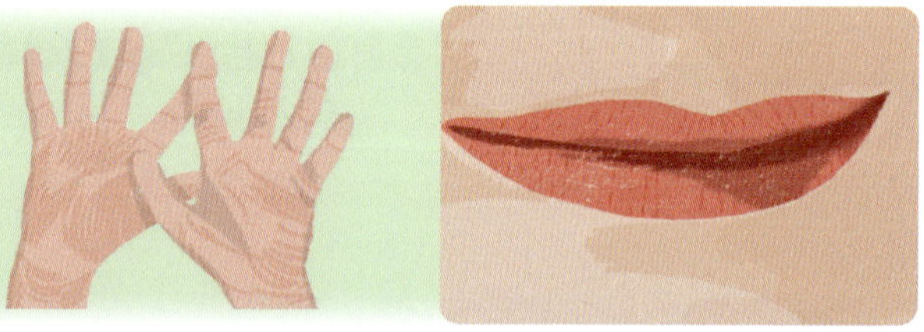

piano		
drums		
recorder		
violin		
guitar		

Think and share!
What's your favourite musical instrument? Can you play it?

4 Watch and listen.

Lesson 7

Accepting or declining an invitation

1 4.17 Read. Then listen and complete.

After-school club

Join my club on ______________ after school!

At the club, you can

- play the guitar ☐
- play tennis ☐
- play board games ☐

Would you like to join my club?

Yes / No

2 Who's joining the club? Read and tick (✓).

Ben ☐ *I'd like to join a tennis club.*

Jack ☐ *I'd like to join a music club.*

Teo ☐ *I'd like to join a football club.*

3 Read and complete.

Join my club!

Name: ______________.

I'd like to play:

tennis / football / drums

the recorder / board games

I can come on:

Mon Tues Wed Thurs Fri

I can shine!

4 Ask and answer.

I can accept or politely decline an invitation.

Let's plan a club!

Step 1 Review

1 Find and write.

2 Look, think and tick (✓) for you.

ride skip swing climb skate kick catch swim

1 ____________ ☐

2 ____________ ☐

3 ____________ ☐

4 ____________ ☐

5 ____________ ☐

6 ____________ ☐

7 ____________ ☐

8 ____________ ☐

3 Ask and answer.

Can he play the guitar?

No, he can't. But he can play board games.

4 What can you do best? Write.

I can ____________.

Step 2 Create

5 Plan your club. Tick (✓).

6 Create a poster for your club. Draw and write.

7 Invite friends to join your club.

Would you like to join my club?

Time to shine!

8 Share your club poster with the class.

Can you skate?

No, I can't but I can swing. I'd like to join your club.

I can try new activities.

Review 2 All about me

1 4.18 Listen and number.

2 Look and point. Then say.

3 Read, match and write.

Yes, I can.	No, I can't.

1 Can you roller skate?

____

2 Can you climb the wall?

____

3 Can you ride a bike?

____

a 

b 

c 

Mini-project

4 Draw and write.

a

Listen to your friend and draw.

There's a ________.

There isn't a ________.

b

Time to shine!

5 Read and tick (✓).

1 I can read and write farm animals and action words. ☐

2 I can talk about farm animals and actions. ☐

3 I can invite friends to a club. ☐

4 I can accept and politely decline an invitation. ☐

6 Vote. Say and sing.

My favourite song is	________ ________
My favourite new word is	________ ________

5 Let's share our food

Lesson 1

Where are the children?

1 5.01 Listen and explore.

Tell me!
What's your favourite vegetable?

2 5.02 Listen, stick and say.

3 Trace and read.

4 Watch and listen.

He's got a carrot.

Lesson 2

1 5.03 Sing and act. Song

What are you doing? I'm eating!
Burgers, carrots, fish and eggs! (x2)
What are you doing? I'm eating!
Cereal, biscuits and oranges, too! (x2)
What are you doing?
I'm drinking orange juice!
I'm drinking orange juice, and so are you!

2 5.05 Listen and tick (✓). Then say.

What are you doing?
I'm eating an orange.

I can shine!

3 Mime, ask and answer.

What are you doing?

I'm eating a burger!

I can name food.

Lesson 3

1 Look at the story. What is Oscar eating? Tick (✓).

soup ☐ a salad ☐ a sandwich ☐ a biscuit ☐

2 5.07 Listen or watch.

 Story value A story about sharing food

Let's imagine!

How are the children helping Stella? How do you think they feel?

I can shine!

3 What's in Clara's soup? Tick (✓).

- a pizza and eggs ☐
- tomatoes and salad ☐
- carrots and tomatoes ☐

4 Act out.

I can understand a story about preparing food.

Lesson 4

1 5.08 Listen and find. **2** 5.09 Listen and number. Say.

3 5.10 Listen, read and say.

Are you cooking?
Yes, I am. / No, I'm not.

Chant

Are you cooking? Are you eating? Yes, I am. Yes, I am!
Are you washing? Are you drinking? No, I'm not. No, I'm not!

4 Follow, read and complete. Ask and answer.

1 Are you ______________ an egg?

2 Are you ______________ tomatoes?

3 Are you ______________ a carrot?

4 Are you ______________ a sandwich?

Lesson 5

1 5.11 Listen and tick (✓). Say.

1 2 3

2 Choose, mime and play. Add one more.

What are you doing?

I'm washing tomatoes!

Are you making a salad?

Yes, I am!

3 5.12 Listen, write and say.

My sounds

An orange in a pot.
A fish on a dish!

I can shine!

4 Cut out, make and play.

Are you cooking?

No, I'm not.
I'm washing the carrots.
I'm making a salad.

I can talk about what I'm doing now.

Lesson 6

1 5.15 Listen, look and find.

2 5.16 Listen and number. Say.

3 Read and circle. Say. Can you add more?

I want...		I need...
pizza		flour butter fruit vegetables ________
sandwich		flour butter fruit vegetables ________
juice		flour butter fruit vegetables ________
soup		flour butter fruit vegetables ________

Think and share!
What food is good for you?

4 Watch and listen.

Lesson 7

Shopping

1 5.17 Read, listen and tick (✓) or cross (✗).

tomatoes ☐
apple juice ☐
eggs ☐
cereal ☐

2 And you? Circle and write.

Shopping list

oranges / apples /
strawberry juice

carrots / tomato soup

____

____

I can shine!

3 Let's go shopping!

I can shop for food.

Let's create a food truck bar!

Step 1 Review

1 Look and write.

2 What food do you like? Tick (✓).

fish burgers carrots oranges juice cereal biscuits eggs

1 ________ ☐
2 ________ ☐
3 ________ ☐
4 ________ ☐
5 ________ ☐
6 ________ ☐
7 ________ ☐
8 ________ ☐

3 Read and complete. Ask and answer.

What are you doing?

1 I'm growing ________.
2 I'm making ________.
3 I'm washing ________.
4 I'm cooking ________.

4 Think! Choose food for your food truck bar.

________ ________ ________

Step 2 Create

5 Write a shopping list.

____

____

____

____

____

____

6 Create your food truck bar poster.

7 Tell your friend what you need.

I need vegetables: tomatoes, carrots and olives!

Time to shine!

8 Share your food poster with the class.

For my food truck I'm making burgers and a salad!

I can share food with friends.

5

6 Let's have holiday fun

Lesson 1

What are they doing?

1 6.01 Listen and explore.

Tell me!
What things can you collect?

2 6.02 Listen, stick and say.

3 Trace and read.

4 Watch and listen.

6 build a sandcastle

Lesson 2

1 6.03 **Sing and act.** Song

I want to play on the beach with my friends (x2)
I want to build a sandcastle!
I want to play on the beach with my friends.

I want to collect shells and rocks. (x2)
I want to swim and climb!
I want to collect shells and rocks.

I want to read comics and sleep. (x2)
I want to have a good time!
I want to read comics and sleep.
I want to go on holiday! (x4)

2 6.05 **Listen and number. Say.**

I want to collect shells!

I can shine!

3 **Choose and say.**

I want to build a sandcastle!

Me, too!

I can name holiday activities.

Lesson 3

1 Look at the story. What is Tess doing? Tick (✓).

- She's reading comics. ☐
- She's building a sandcastle. ☐
- She's collecting shells. ☐

2 6.07 Listen or watch.

Rise and Shine

Explorers Club

 Story value A story about working together to help others

I can shine!

Let's imagine!

Who turns the Club into the beach? Why?

3 Who says what? Write, match and say.

collect build play

1 I want to __________ football.

2 I want to __________ shells.

3 I want to __________ a sandcastle.

Clara

Tess

Oscar

4 Act out.

I can understand a story about holiday activities.

Lesson 4

1 6.08 Listen and find.

2 6.09 Listen and tick (✓). Say.

3 6.10 Listen, read and say.

Do you want to play?
Yes, I do. / No, I don't.

Chant

Do you want to play in the morning? Yes, I do!
Do you want to play in the afternoon? Yes, I do!
Do you want to play in the evening? Yes, I do!
Do you want to play at night? No, I don't! I want to sleep!

4 Follow, choose and write. Ask and answer.

1 Do you want to ______________________ in the morning?

2 Do you want to ______________ in the ______________?

3 Do you want to ______________________ in _____ evening?

Lesson 5

1 6.11 Listen and match. Then tick (✓) for you and say.

morning | afternoon | evening

2 Choose, mime and play.

Do you want to collect shells in the morning?

Yes, I do.

3 6.12 Listen, write and say.

My sounds

u

e

The sun is out, let's have fun.
It's cold and wet, let's go to bed!

I can shine!

4 Cut out, ask and answer.

Do you want to ride a bike?

Yes, I do! I want to ride a bike in the afternoon. Do you want to play football?

I can talk about what I want to do on holiday.

Lesson 6

1 6.15 Listen, look and find. **2** 6.16 Listen and number.

sea | flag | safe | dangerous

3 Look and write *S* (safe) or *D* (dangerous). Say.

1

3

2

4

Think and share!
Do you prefer cold or hot weather on holiday?

4 Watch and listen.

Lesson 7

Going on holiday

1 6.17 Listen and read. Then circle.

Dear Grandad,

This holiday is great!
I'm playing on the beach, building sandcastles and swimming in the sea. The weather is hot and sunny.

Miss you,

Jake

2 Read and complete.

Dear __________,

I like / don't like my holiday!

The weather is __________ and __________.

I'm __________ and __________.

See you soon,

____

I can shine!

3 Let's go on holiday!

I can talk about my holiday.

Let's plan a holiday trip!

Step 1 Review

1 Find and write. **2 What activities do you like? Tick (✓).**

comics holiday build shells collect sandcastles beach sleep

1 go on __________ ☐

2 ______________________ ☐

3 play on the __________ ☐

4 __________ __________ ☐

5 read __________ ☐

6 __________ __________ ☐

3 Read and complete. Ask and answer.

1 In the morning, I want to ______________

____________________________________.

2 In the afternoon, I want to ____________

____________________________________.

Do you want to sleep on holiday?

4 Choose and say.

 ☐  ☐

I like ________ weather on holiday.

Step 2 Create

5 Think of activities. Write.

Monday

Morning ____________________

Afternoon __________________

Tuesday

Morning ____________________

Afternoon __________________

6 Create your holiday trip plan. Draw and write.

7 Describe your holiday trip plan.

I want to sleep in the afternoon!

Time to shine!

8 Share your holiday trip plan with the class.

Do you want to play on the beach?

Yes, I do. I want to play on the beach in the morning.

I can plan holiday fun with friends.

Review 3 Around me

1 6.18 Listen and number.

2 Look and point. Then ask and answer.

3 Read, write and match.

collect build read

1 I want to ______________________ a sandcastle. ☐

2 I want to ______________________ shells. ☐

3 I want to ______________________ a comic. ☐

Mini-project

4 Create a sign for the Explorers Club.

Time to shine!

5 Read and tick (✓).

1 I can read and write food and holiday words. ☐

2 I can talk about food and holiday activities. ☐

3 I can ask what people are doing. ☐

4 I can talk about what I want to do. ☐

6 Vote. Say and sing.

My favourite song is	______________ ______________
My favourite new word is	______________ ______________

Goodbye from the Explorers Club

What is Oscar doing?

1 7.01 Listen and explore.

2 7.02 Listen again and tick (✓).

3 Watch.

4 7.03 **Sing and act.** Song

Goodbye, Stella, Tess and Clara,
Basil, Oscar and Peanut, too!
It's holiday time and I'm an explorer!
Lots of things to see and do!
Goodbye! Goodbye!
Happy holiday to you!

I can shine!

5 **Draw you as an explorer. Then say.**

I'm an explorer! I want to…

What a great picture!

Level 2

Test your progress with English Benchmark Young Learners

Let them shine!

What can you see?

1 8.01 Listen and number. Say.

2 8.02 Sing and act. Listen again and circle. Song

It's your birthday, let's have fun!
A cake and a sparkler for everyone!
Happy birthday, happy birthday, happy birthday to you!
A watch, a backpack, a book and a ball!
Thank you for my presents! I like them all!
Happy birthday, happy birthday, happy birthday to you!

3 Make a sparkler decoration.

Have you got a sparkler?

Yes, I have. Look!

Beautiful world

What can you see?

1 8.05 Listen and number. Say.

2 8.06 Sing and act. Listen again and circle.

Song

This is a beautiful world! How can it be?
Turtles in the ocean and fish in the sea!
Animals on mountains and hills and in trees!
This is a beautiful world! Do you know why?
Animals in the jungle, in the desert, in the sky!

3 Make a beautiful world.

I love the ocean!

I like mountains!

Amazing oceans

What can you see?

1 8.09 Listen and number. Say.

2 8.10 Sing and act. Song

What can you see in the ocean?
At the bottom of the deep blue sea?
Can you see a seahorse?
Yes! Yes! Yes!
I can see a seahorse, an octopus,
a dolphin and a seal!
A shark and a whale – at the
bottom of the deep blue sea!

Ocean animals which start with the letter *s*:

____

____

____

3 Make an ocean scene.

What's in your ocean?

There's an octopus!

Let them fly!

What can you see?

1 Listen and number. Say.

2 Sing and act. Listen again and write *D* (day) or *N* (night).

Song

I'm flying a kite.
I can see the sun!
I can see clouds in the sky!
It's day and I'm flying a kite.
Fly, kite, fly!
I'm flying a kite.
I can see the moon.
I can see stars in the sky.
It's night and I'm flying a kite.
Fly, kite, fly!

sun	☐	clouds	☐
moon	☐	stars	☐

3 Make a kite.

I like your kite!

Thank you!

Pearson Education Limited
KAO Two
KAO Park
Hockham Way
Harlow, Essex
CM17 9SR
England
and Associated Companies throughout the world.

pearsonenglish.com

First published 2021

Fourth impression 2024

ISBN: 978-1-292-36929-7

Set in Daytona Pro Primary

Printed in Slovakia by Neografia

Acknowledgements
The publisher would like to thank the following for their kind permission to reproduce their photographs:

(Key: b-bottom c-centre l-left r-right t-top)

123RF.com: Cathy Yeulet 17, Krystian Krawczyk 27; **Getty Images:** 26, Alberto Manuel Urosa Toledano 70, Alejandro Ascanio/EyeEm 60, Alex Levine 26, Arnuphap Yaiphimai/EyeEm 70, Ascent Xmedia 16, Claudiu Maxim/EyeEm 17, Colin Hawkins 38, Drazen_ 71, Emma Innocenti 17, Flottmynd 70, Hill Street Studios 17, JGI/Jamie Grill 48, Jose Luis Pelaez Inc 19, kuppa_rock 60, LWA 17, ManuelVelasco 26, Marc Romanelli 17, Marco Bottigelli 70, MarsYu 38, Matthias Tunger 16, MILATAS 27, Peter Cade 16, 70, Peter Dazeley 27, Pho Ton 38, PhotoAlto 38, ra-photos 26, SergeiKorolko 9, 31, 53, 75; Stephen Gibson/EyeEm 60, susan.k. 48, SVGiles 38, Westend61 16, yulkapopkova 71; **Pearson Education Ltd:** Jon Barlow 7, 9, 15, 19, 25, 27, 29, 37, 39, 41, 47, 49, 51, 59, 61, 63, 69, 71, 73, 78, 79, 80, 81; **Shutterstock.com:** Arteck555 48, BBA Photography 38, Cara-Foto 60, Good Shop Background 48, Kateryna Mashkevych 70, Photographee.eu 27, Pixel-Shot 27, PunkbarbyO 8, Tatiana Popova 71, Yurchenko Yulia 14

Cover image: Alamy Stock Photo/Zoonar GmbH with course characters (illustrated by BluBlu Studios)

All other images © Pearson Education

Illustrated by BluBlu Studios (course characters); Denis Cristo / Sylvie Poggio: pp. 14, 25, 36, 58; Becky Down/The Bright Agency: pp. 30, 31, 52, 53, 74, 75, 82-91; Megan Higgins /The Bright Agency: pp. 28, 29, 50, 51, 62; Julie Ingham/The Bright Agency pp: 38, 39, 46, 48; Edyta Karaban/Sylvie Poggio: pp. 78-81; Adam Linley/Beehive Illustration: pp. 5 (calendar) 11, 21, 33, 43, 55, 65, (all I can Shine sticker artworks); Stepph Marshall/The Bright Agency: pp. 9, 16, 26, 60, 61; Alex Naidoo/Sylvie Poggio: pp.15, 25, 37, 47, 59, 68, 69; Lucy Neale/The Bright Agency: pp. 18, 19, 40, 41, 72; Mark Ruffle /Beehive Illustration: pp. 4 (Explorer's badge), 6, 7, 9, 12, /15, 25, 37, 47, 59, 69 my sounds.

https://www.un.org/sustainabledevelopment/
The content of this publication has not been approved by the United Nations and does not reflect the views of the United Nations or its officials or Member States.

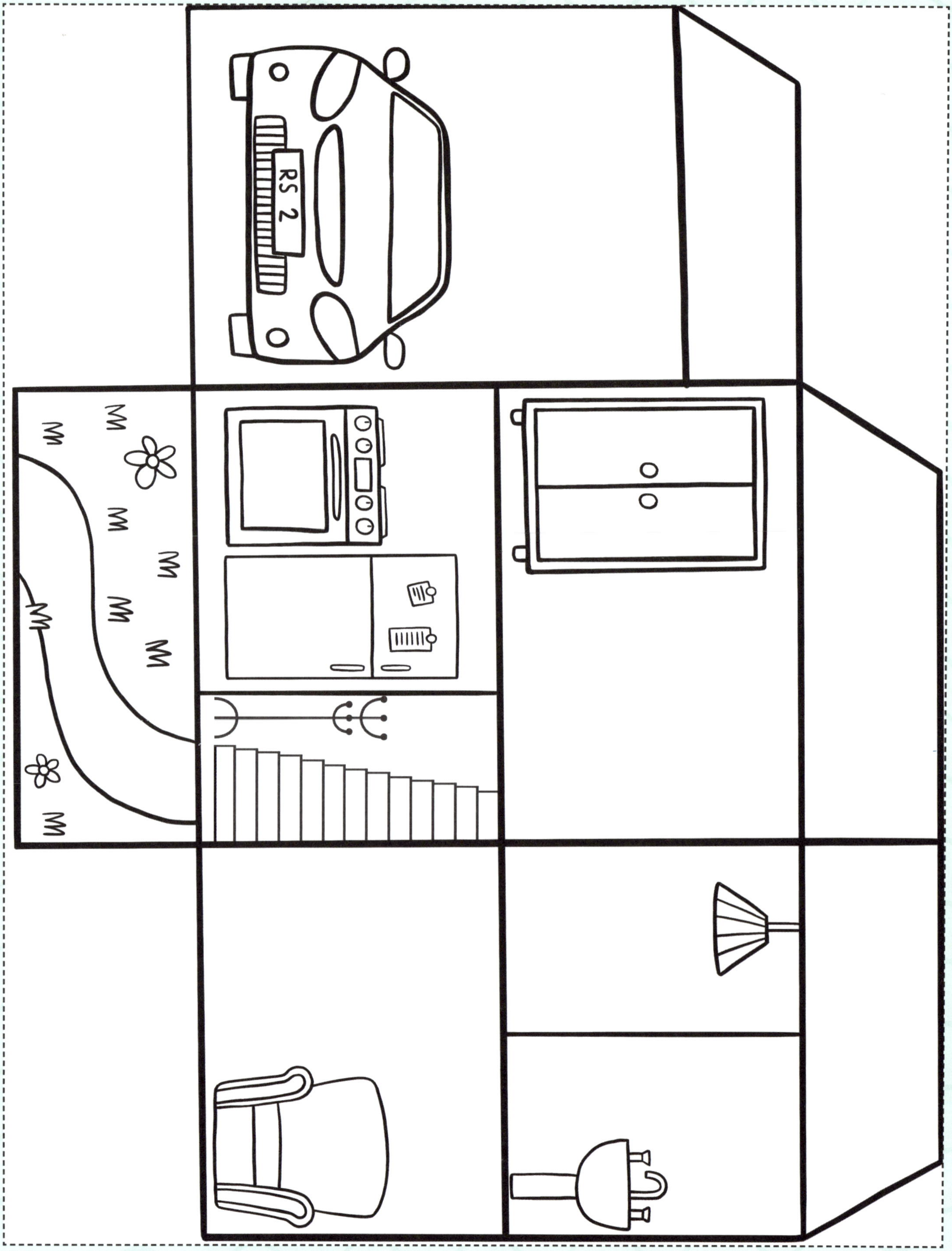
RS 2

Name:
Swim
play the guitar
CLIMB
Skate
PLAY FOOTBALL

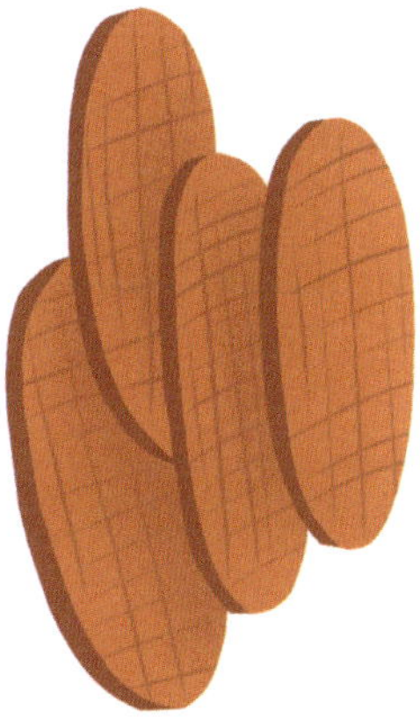

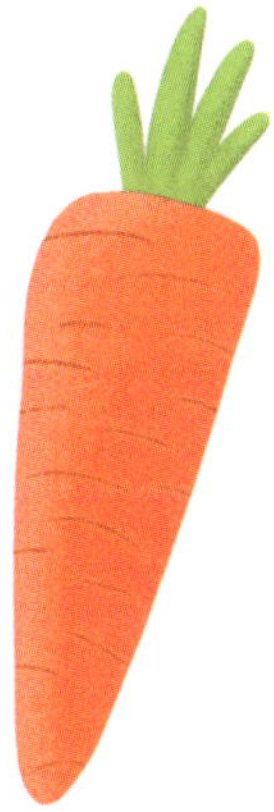

SUPER
BOY
KIDS FUN

Rise and Shine stickers

Welcome

Unit 1

pages 10–11

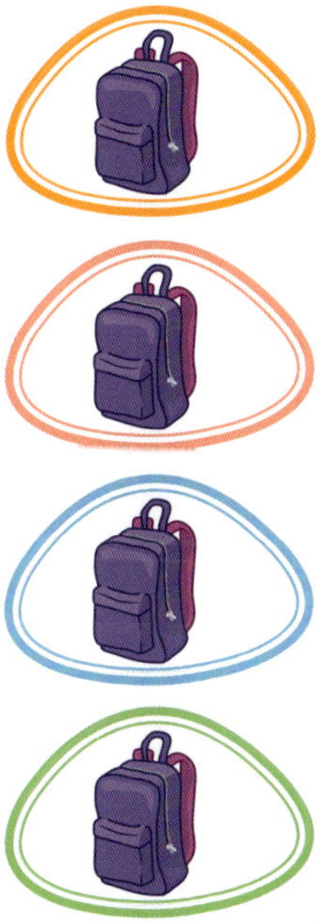

Unit 2

pages 20–21

Unit 3

pages 32–33

Unit 4

pages 42–43

Unit 5

pages 54–55

pages 64–65

Unit 6

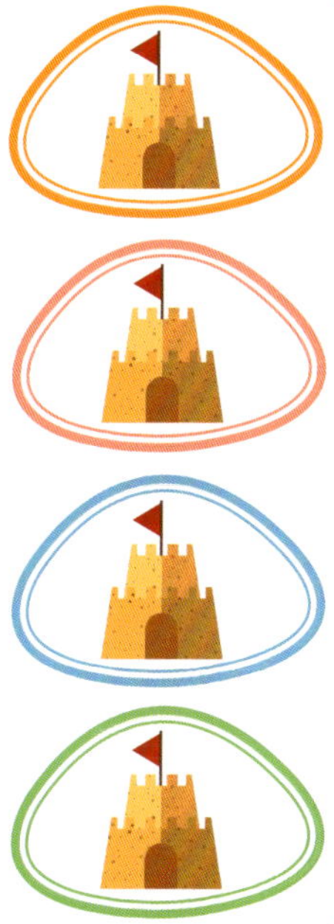